Positive Thinking

A Comprehensive 28-Day Program Designed To Enhance
Self-development By Addressing Negative Thinking,
Anxiety, And Poor Motivation Through The Cultivation Of
A Positive Mindset

TORSTEN SCHULZ

TABLE OF CONTNET

Give Yourself A Break: Reasons Why You Must Choose Happiness... 1

Management Of Strong, Quick-Acting Intention Statements 15

Principles First 32

Ten Ugly Thoughts Everyone Has And How To Fix Them 44

A Mindset Of Abundance And Gratitude 63

Managing Disgusting Trauma 80

Appropriate Ways To Do Affirmations? 103

Create A Structural Area Around You 114

Successful Visualization Techniques 136

Establishing A Creative Settlement 157

Give Yourself A Break: Reasons Why You Must Choose Happiness.

There's no denying that modern life may be hectic and overstimulating. Because of this, a lot of people now routinely deal with stress, headaches, and sleep deprivation. Most people find them uncomfortable even if they can't get out of these circumstances.

In actuality, many people commit suicide—both physically and psychologically—in an attempt to keep up with the hectic pace of contemporary life. The "feverishly accelerated" pace of today may give rise to serious mental illnesses such as chronic fatigue and unhappiness.

We must learn coping strategies to deal with the stress and worry of living in the modern world. For a significant part, for example, the author often felt overwhelmed by the burden of bustling modern life, particularly in big cities like New York. He found that he could let go of that anxiety by setting aside time to go for walks in the woods.

Ultimately, our discontent with these conditions is a choice that we can change or undo. The truth is that real socioeconomic conditions like unemployment or poverty can contribute to unhappiness.

But these conditions are not as important as our views about them, which can empower us to choose happiness in the face of adversity or deepen our despair. If selected, melancholy could start a vicious cycle where negativity feeds on more negativity.

Since they are not "super-sophisticated," children are "happiness experts," they have not yet learned that society wants them to be miserable. They are this concept's real-life incarnation.

IDEAS 7

Never give up: why it's important to constantly try to see the good in situations where difficulties arise.

Have you ever shown up at an important meeting unprepared? That's a horrible feeling, isn't it? We must prepare for anything that might come up, but if we mentally prepare for the worst, we are more likely to run into problems.

In actuality, you stop the power flow when you imagine the worst-case scenarios, which reduces your ability to overcome obstacles. Even if you go beyond these obstacles, your negative mindset will demonstrate that you lack the strength to do so.

How we tackle these obstacles dictates our course of action. If we believe they can be controlled, they will be!

One example of this is the well-known tennis player from the 1940s, Pancho Gonzalez. Even though he wasn't the greatest player and was undoubtedly an outsider, he yet managed to win numerous championships during his playing career.

How did he manage to do that? He never let himself become discouraged in the face of defeat; instead, he continually looked for and pursued prospects for success.

And we can solve every problem this way since there are no intractable problems. Just keep an optimistic outlook and recognize the opportunities at your disposal.

Certainly, your mind is attempting to tell you that there are problems you just can't seem to address. You could, nevertheless, train your thoughts to be more optimistic. Changing how you convey the possible outcomes of your life to emphasize its positive aspects instead of its negative ones is one way to do this.

Again, mental "draining" is essential in this scenario since it helps you concentrate on the achievable and resolve your problems by purging your mind of negative outcomes.

There are often multiple solutions to a particular problem, which you may not find on your first attempt. If your mind is clear and your attention is on the positive, your chances of spotting them are much higher.

Engage in mindfulness exercises.

Focus on the here and now without evaluation, appraisal, or analysis. Choose a quiet place to sit and push away any thoughts that come to mind without judging them as good or negative.

Inhale. Breathing can quickly improve your mood. Pay attention to your breathing to become more adept at being actively attentive. Make an effort to pay attention to the actual feelings of air entering and leaving your body.

Your body will undoubtedly feel more tranquil after taking a few breaths. Now that you're in this state of peace, your brain will naturally begin to slow down.

Try out several attentive activities.

Consider mindfulness exercises and meditation to be mental workouts. You can attempt the following methods of meditation: - Mental body scans. Start from the tips of your toes and concentrate on different body areas.

- As you approach the top of your head, gradually move your attention to the next body area. Instead of tensing or manipulating your muscles, concentrate on the sensations in each region of your body and ignore ideas that label those sensations.

- Take up walking meditation. Be mindful of the physical aspects of every stride, such as the sensation of your feet hitting the ground, the cadence and pattern of your breathing, and the breeze caressing your skin.

- You then eat with awareness. Take a seat at a table and focus on your meal. Put your phone aside and refrain from watching or reading anything. Eat mindfully, paying attention to the taste and feel of every meal.

Another option is to engage in transient mindfulness. You will notice shifts in your mind when you integrate mindfulness with your mental attitude. Additionally, you can amp up their impact by recognizing the good influences when they occur. Observe when you: -enjoy regular daily routines. Enjoyable moments come from engaging in ritual conduct. Spend time with your pet when you arrive home, or spend time over your morning tea or after lunch on a stroll around the block. Even though they might not seem like much, they can bring stability and serenity if done consistently.

-focus on one task at a time. Multitasking all the time is easily the result of modern living. As a result, one finds it nearly impossible to focus entirely on one item. You must focus on one thing to be as productive, enjoyable, and focused as possible.

-cling to happy recollections.

Realistic goal-setting and accomplishment

- Make sure your daily objectives are clear and doable. Establish objectives based on your self-improvement or self-care, such as going to bed sooner. Maintain a consistent sleep routine and fight the urge to nap on days when you don't have to get up early. Getting adequate sleep will improve your emotional stability, reduce your susceptibility to stress, increase your productivity, and improve your decision-making ability. Aim for seven to nine hours per night of sleep.

- Work out. Five days per week. Health specialists encourage moderate exercise to improve mental well-being, and it can alleviate anxiety and sadness. Choose pursuits that you find enjoyable.

Advantages of physical activity: stronger thinking and enhanced memory. Endorphins are released during activity. Aid in concentration.

Enhanced self-worth

More vitality and better sleep.

You'll possess mental toughness.

- Lighten up on the workload. According to studies, those who prioritize their time over money have happier lives and better manage their finances. At work, set difficult yet attainable goals. Additionally, doing any necessary basic activities before the end of the workday will help you unwind.

Make connections with other people.

Spend time with upbeat folks.

You have to acknowledge that the people you surround yourself with greatly impact you. You might be shocked to hear that spending time with loved ones and maintaining strong personal relationships are the best indicators of happiness rather than having a lot of money or being in good health.

-go out and discover what brings you greater joy than worldly belongings. This is a result of people sharing their experiences. Make prudent use of your spare time and discretionary cash.

- Cut off ties with individuals who treat you disrespectfully and don't encourage you. Being close without love is a surefire way to end up sad.

Boost the number of good deeds you do.

When you conduct sporadic acts of civility, be honest. Research has indicated that you get a positive emotional response when you go above and above in a favor. This is because you will be more appreciative if you do this instead of just acting kindly without feeling anything when you do it.

You will make others and yourself happy if you practice kindness with sincerity.

Offer assistance

Put yourself in a situation where you can engage with people positively. You will be making someone else's day better, and you will also be making your own. Your feeling of purpose will be restored, your social isolation will decrease, and your self-confidence will increase due to volunteering. You can volunteer at community centers for the elderly, libraries, and animal shelters.

Talk to someone younger than you.

Younger individuals are happier than older adults, according to research. Spend time with the kids.

Management Of Strong, Quick-Acting Intention Statements

The purpose of the subsequent phases is to formulate strong, immediate intentions. They are essential since they are the cornerstones that will guarantee favorable outcomes. Let's examine them and discover how they can significantly alter and enhance your life.

[1] You Need to State Your Intention in the Present Tense

Since the subconscious mind has no past or future, intention statements must be expressed in the present tense. From the subconscious's perspective, events from the past can be brought back to life in the present by repeating them in your mind. You must stop repeatedly playing your old tapes because of this. Your subconscious believes you have gone through the same thing more than once when you act that way.

It is best to express your objectives in the present tense by avoiding the use of phrases like "someday," "soon," or "tomorrow." You want to develop the habit of believing that whatever you are visualizing and affirming is happening in your mind at that same moment.

Forms are produced from ideas. This implies that accepting a concept in the present tense will cause it to materialize quickly as you are embracing it in this manner. It is important to note that the speed at which the desired outcome materializes or is achieved depends on our capacity to accept what we are visualizing and affirming. All is dependent upon our degree of acceptance. Your subconscious will act on your intentions immediately if you maintain them in the present tense, which means you accept them there.

[2] You Should Express What You WANT in Your Intention Statement Rather Than What You DON'T Want.

The emphasis of intentions should be on gaining rather than losing. Don't explain what you are attempting to eliminate or move away from. As an alternative, declare your progress. The idea is to focus your intentions and images on what you want to achieve rather than what you want to give up or run away from.

I have noticed that a lot of people employ REVERSE INTENTIONS. They affirm what they don't want rather than what they want.

You must say what you want in your intention statement, not what you feel you "should" want.

For instance, your mother said, "You should become a doctor." Which is it—a "should" or a "want"? It is a "should" unless you want to be a doctor.

If you start to lose interest in carrying out your intention statement, it's the best indicator that it is a "should" rather than a "want." If so, you are most likely confirming a "should" rather than a "want."

The issue is that most individuals don't know what they want, so they create negative outcomes rather than great ones.

It amazes me how many of my coaching clients find it difficult to articulate their desires in a response when I ask them, "What do you want?"

At most, they can generally think of a way to improve their current circumstance or something they don't want. They accomplish this by drawing parallels.

They use terms like "better," "more," etc. As an illustration, "I want to feel better."

"I wish to have greater self-assurance."

"I wish I had more money," and so on.

That is not as good as confirming the bad, but the disadvantage is that it always subtly draws attention to something bad they don't want. Put differently, it highlights the things that their goal is meant to be "better" than or "more" of. This negates the entire purpose of creating the intention statement in the first place by keeping the worst-case scenario in their minds.

I'll give you an illustration.

When I ask clients what they want to get rid of in their lives, they can usually describe it to me in great detail. They'll remark, "I want my boyfriend to stop hanging out with his friends so much."

Or, "I'm aware that I don't want a job that requires me to travel a lot."

This is because, in their minds, they will have a very distinct picture of what they like and dislike and very little, or at most, a hazy picture of what they would like to have. Put another way, their deep obsession is typically with what they don't have or what is wrong in their lives.

Regretfully, this is a completely incorrect approach to establishing a successful intention. You will keep experiencing your current scenario repeatedly if you preserve a negative mental image of the things you don't want or enjoy about it. This is because you are cementing the unpleasant situation into your memory.

Focusing on what you want instead of what you don't want will lead to that end if you can visualize a good outcome that will solve your problem. There's a strong chance you will draw that outcome into your life.

Why does this matter?

This is because, as you are surely aware, a computer thinks in literal terms, and your subconscious mind functions similarly to a computer. It's important to ask precise questions while using a computer to enter data and discover the solution to a specific issue. Your brain functions in the same manner as your subconscious mind.

It interprets incoming data literally, much like all other computers do. The accuracy of the commands it receives determines how well it performs or what happens in the end. It needs to comprehend the instruction, or else it won't know what to do!

Consequently, your computer mind does not comprehend when you say that you want to "do better in school" or use any other comparable expression. The term "doing better" might signify anything to your computer mind. It could imply performing significantly better or simply marginally better.

The issue is that your subconscious isn't aware of the difference between "doing better in school" and receiving an A or a C+. From the perspective of your computer mind, a C is preferable to a C+.

Therefore, an unclear intention declaration will lead to an uncertain consequence.

5 Living Present-Moment: Developing Mindfulness for a Happy Life

Being mindful is a meaningful habit that greatly improves our mental health; it's more than just a catchphrase. A 2011 Psychosomatic Medicine study states mindfulness can lower stress and enhance general health. It's about living in the moment and savoring the little pleasures in life without letting regrets from the past or anxieties about the future get in the way. Although it originated in early Buddhist meditation, its applicability is universal and transcends all religions and cultures. It takes time and practice to become attentive, like learning to play an instrument.

It's not as hard as you would believe to incorporate mindfulness into your regular practice. For example, mindful breathing focuses on your breath and can be practiced at any time or place. For this reason, apps such as Calm provide guided breathing exercises. Though it may sound corny, taking deep breaths is a great approach to finding your core. Your rest-and-digest system is triggered, which helps you unwind right away. These and other more specialized exercises will be covered in later chapters.

Another useful strategy is mindful eating, which encourages more enjoyment and healthier eating practices by requiring the participant to completely participate in the meal. In addition to practicing awareness, chewing each bite 20 times helps you concentrate on the flavor and texture of your food. An effective weight-maintenance strategy was associated with this practice in participants in a University of California, San Francisco study. Regular chores like cleaning or driving can be transformed into occasions to practice mindfulness. These tasks take on new meaning when one concentrates on their feelings and experiences, transcending them from simple tasks.

The Relationship Between Positive Thought and Mindfulness

Positive thought and mindfulness go hand in hand. Positive events are fully appreciated when we focus on the here and now. Dealing with negative ideas can also be healthy when mindfulness is practiced. Through mindfulness, we learn to watch these ideas without passing judgment on them instead of becoming caught in them or attempting to repress them. This method lessens the effect of negative ideas on our general positivity by enabling us to respond to them in a balanced manner. I frequently employ the CBT approach of "letting hard emotions wash over me" while imagining myself beneath a waterfall. Negative ideas will come and go much more swiftly if you don't repress them. You can digest them more quickly. Negative thoughts and sensations are merely made to linger longer by emotional repression (as well as mental disengagement from life's challenges). Accept the darkness; it will pass quickly. The greatest advantage of mindfulness is this. Feelings of negativity come over you and then swiftly pass.

Incorporating mindfulness into your daily life is essential to fully benefit from it. You may take a slower lunch break, begin your day with mindful breathing, or finish it with a quick meditation session. Numerous guided mindfulness exercises appropriate for various schedules and tastes can be found in apps like Insight Timer. It takes constancy to develop this habit; at first, it's typical for the mind to stray. Refocusing gradually is crucial whenever you observe this occurring.

Recall that practicing mindfulness can make a big difference in your life, even for a little while each day. By using this skill, we may better enjoy the present moment and manage our thoughts and emotions. We expose ourselves to a life with greater awareness and serenity as we investigate and incorporate mindfulness into our daily lives.

Principles First

In this chapter, he presents the first rule of wealth accumulation, which states that the cosmos is a thinking entity that reacts to mental energy. He contends that one can draw prosperity and abundance into one's life by directing one's thoughts in a way consistent with the universe's creative force. He contends that this idea is the cornerstone of all prosperity and success.

The Influence of Thought

He starts by highlighting that thought is the origin of all creation.

"Everything in our universe, both physical and visible, started off as an idea in someone's head. Our reality is created and shaped by the power of thinking. Our own fate is something we have designed."

He contends that the capacity for thought and the capacity to visualize one's desired results are the foundations of all prosperity and success. He contends that one might start drawing prosperity and abundance into one's life by visualizing it.

The cosmos as a substance capable of thought

Next, Frankie presents the idea that the universe is a sentient being. He claims: "The universe is a thinking power of our thoughts. It is a living, breathing organism that reacts to the power of thought." Our thoughts and beliefs directly influence our reality and the experiences we encounter in life."

He says that one can draw prosperity and success into one's life by directing one's thoughts in a way consistent with the universe's creative force.

The Attraction Law

Frankie talks about the law of attraction, which says that similar things attract similar things. He contends that one might draw chances and experiences akin to this into their lives by thinking positively and abundantly: "According to the focus our attention and energy on. We can draw prosperity and prosperity into our life by thinking positive and plentiful thoughts."

He encourages readers to let go of self-limiting ideas and skills and to concentrate on forming a precise and distinct picture of their intended results. He says that by doing this, one can start drawing in the opportunities and resources required to bring those results to pass.

Expressing gratitude and using imagery

Frankie stresses the value of visualization and thankfulness in bringing one's thoughts into harmony with the universe's creative force. He says that one can manifest their desired outcomes by visualizing them and expressing appreciation for what they already have. "Gratitude and visualization are powerful tools for harnessing the creative power of the universe," he says. We can draw our desired outcomes into our lives by clearly and precisely visualizing them and acknowledging and appreciating what we already have."

He says that one can create a more pleasant and abundant life by concentrating on what they want rather than what they don't want.

The Power of Positive Thinking in Chapter One

Welcome to the first volume of our investigation into the science behind the sciencey portions of positive thinking and its wonders.

Positive Thinking: A Wonder of Psychology

We begin our adventure together by delving into the human psyche. With an infinite amount of storage, the capacity to retrieve information faster than a Lamborgini at full speed, and the ability to light a lightbulb for all those...lightbulb moments, the human mind is a truly amazing piece of engineering. Your brain can rewire as an internal IT helpdesk that speaks your language. This is known as neuroplasticity, and it makes your brain highly flexible. Very cool! This implies that it is capable of learning, healing from wounds, and adjusting to novel circumstances and experiences as they arise. When used in the alchemy of positive thought, it can also evoke amazing changes because the fundamental function of positive thinking is to initiate a significant change in the mental terrain of our minds. It's like letting the aroma of fish and chips fill a stifling room by prying open the windows.

Let's now get into the specifics of psychology. Though it's coming a little closer, positive thinking is more than a nice, fuzzy sensation after a Scotch and American. It also doesn't only mean glowing after fantastic sex. It's not just a transient mood swing like "Hey, today I will be less grumpy"; rather, it's a complete way of looking at life that can drastically alter your reality. Researchers in long white coats have been studying this stuff for years. After much writing and discussion—possibly concurrently—they came to the conclusion that thinking positively, perhaps about amazing sex, causes your brain to produce a wave of feel-good neurotransmitters like serotonin and dopamine. This neurochemical mixture produces a happy, stress-relieving, smokeless atmosphere similar to the sparks that light up a fireworks display inside our brains.

For example, You wake up at six in the morning to the Power Rangers theme song that your phone somehow downloaded a few days ago. The alarm on your phone won't go off for an unknown reason, even to the manufacturers. You poke and swipe aimlessly, still not understanding the intricacies of the snooze feature, until "Go Go Power Rangers, Mighty Morphin' Power Rangers" abruptly gives up. Now that you're fully awake, another workday is calling. You could give in to the allure of pessimism as you lay back in the calming silence, or you could decide to turn away from the past five years and adopt optimistic thoughts for the day ahead. Your brain will instantly react favorably—and perhaps unexpectedly—by rewarding you with a massive dopamine rush that will instantly make you feel energized, driven, and prepared to take on the day's problems. This is the neurological science of positivity at work in your bed, not just wishful thinking!

Neuroplasticity: The Amazing Flexibility of the Brain

I then brought up neuroplasticity and the idea that our brains are dynamic, incredibly adaptive structures rather than static ones. The master builder working behind the scenes, neuroplasticity, rearranges the furniture in our brains to make room for our ideas and experiences. Imagine it as a huge ball of playdough if that's any use.

When we constantly practice, positive thinking creates new neural pathways in our brains. We reinforce existing pathways and create new ones every time we consciously choose to think positively, making it simpler to rely on optimism and resilience. Positive thinking is a cognitive ability we may develop over time rather than merely a transient feeling. Anyone and everyone can incorporate it into their thoughts and behaviors if they have the necessary knowledge and abilities. That includes you, too.

The Effect of Ripples

Let's now explore the social implications of positive thinking by going outside the boundaries of our imaginations. Positive energy radiates forth from our individual experiences. The effect resembles throwing a pebble into a pond and seeing how the ripples spread, impacting everyone nearby.

This has the potential to significantly alter any situation. Let's say you've managed to get out of bed and arrive at work. You discover that the project your team is working on has extremely demanding deadlines. Rather than giving in to negativity and moaning about everything, you deliberately keep a positive outlook while looking for possibilities and solutions to advance quickly. Your positive attitude spreads to your coworkers, inspiring them to pursue the assignment with more zeal and determination. The office immediately becomes more peaceful and productive for everyone, including those wearing skimpy pants..

Ten Ugly Thoughts Everyone Has And How To Fix Them

I'll never forget when I realized how much my self-talk affected every part of my life and heard that for the first time. Our negative ideas and inner dialogue can be very restrictive, and we can be our worst enemies. I was unaware of this basic information, as most people do.

After a while, I saw that my negative beliefs were self-imposed constraints that I placed on myself, which I could easily remove. Over the past ten years, I've realized that most of us genuinely have similar negative ideas. These are some of the most typical negative thoughts we all experience, along with some solutions.

1. I am insufficient. Have you ever felt inadequate or unworthy? When we believe we are unworthy. This feeling of self-doubt and pity drowns us. It may indicate a low sense of self-worth, although everyone is deserving.

Even though you might not currently possess the abilities or resources to realize your goals, you are unquestionably competent and deserving of obtaining your desired outcomes. Does a fifty-dollar bill lose its worth if it falls on cow poop? Naturally, no! Why, therefore, do you think your life experiences diminish your worth?

Solutions. Tell yourself that you are worthy of whatever you want in this life, just like everyone else, rather than thinking, "I am not good enough." Now, concentrate on the positive aspects of who you are. If seeing the list daily helps, you can write it down and stick it somewhere handy.

2. I'm not capable of that. One of the most restrictive phrases you may say to yourself is "can't." "Whether you think you can or can't, you are right," Henry

Ford famously stated. You are telling your mind and brain that you cannot, and that is what you will experience if you tell yourself that you cannot. If you have already convinced your mind that something is impossible, it will not attempt it.

Solutions. Remind yourself that you can accomplish anything you set your mind to rather than concentrating your negative thoughts on what you believe is impossible. Even if everyone has limitations, believing in your ability is the first step to reaching your short- and long-term life goals.

And occasionally, you might only require a modest pick-me-up. Obtain the worksheet for an instant motivation boost. A worksheet designed to help you find inspiration by encouraging you to do the small things.

3. I'm not as fortunate as other folks. This thinking usually stems from the delusion that you are better off than others because of their better lifestyles and greater luck. "Perfect" is unattainable, and apparent "luck" frequently results after much work.

Believing that you will never experience happiness in life is incredibly demoralizing; yet, if you practice thankfulness, you will discover that happiness is already present everywhere you look.

Solutions. Remind yourself that good things can and will happen to you rather than concentrating on all the luck that other people seem to enjoy. To see all the positive things you would otherwise miss, practice thankfulness. For instance, when did you last appreciate your comfortable bed, the food in your refrigerator, or the roof over your head?

4. I doubt I ever will. It's true that anything you think will come to pass. Every day, the decisions you make and the habits you develop will determine your future. You can undermine your chances by putting limitations on yourself through pessimistic ideas.

Imagine what it would be like to think you could achieve your true goals and have the experiences you have always wanted. Things are more important to try than to get things perfect the first time. Never give up on yourself before you've even given yourself an opportunity.

Solutions. Don't let self-limiting beliefs that suggest you'll never succeed in your goals constrain you. Say to yourself, "I am confident I will," instead. Despite your lack of confidence, positive thinking will gradually increase your self-assurance.

5. My performance should be higher. When the word "should" is used this way, it creates a negative mindset and makes the person feel inferior. How often do you tell yourself, "I should be more productive, intelligent, disciplined,

etc. than I am"? Recall your immediate post-event feelings.

Solutions. "I am trying to change what I don't like," tell yourself. Everyone has areas of themselves they would like to do better at, and it is feasible to do so as long as you approach the task with patience and self-love.

Establish goals for the aspects of your life you are unhappy with rather than telling yourself what you "should" look like or do. Make the changes you want to see happen, and get rid of any morally restrictive terms from your lexicon.

6. My strength is insufficient. Feeling like you're not strong enough is common. I don't know anyone who

doesn't feel weak because we are all human. But what matters is the discussion you have with yourself afterward. How can you expect to feel if you always think negative thoughts reinforcing your lack of strength?

Solutions. Tell yourself that you are strong enough to handle the problems ahead of you rather than dwelling on your shortcomings, and help yourself discover the strength you require at that moment.

7. No one is concerned. Even though it may seem that no one is interested in you and you are alone, I do not doubt that there are people out there thinking about you. People are sensitive; however, not everyone shows their

feelings similarly. Quit concentrating on the unpleasant sense that no one is interested in you, and quit assuming things about other people you don't know. Instead, shift your attention to something that improves your mood.

Solutions. Remind yourself that there are individuals in your life who genuinely care about you rather than assuming that no one does. To counter your negative ideas, try your best to nurture those relationships and embrace the love that comes from others.

8. I'm not very intelligent. Even though this is a fairly general statement, many individuals say it frequently and then feel self-conscious about it later. What specifically are you not smart at? If

I asked you to list several areas in which you excel, I'm sure you could if you put in the effort.

Since nobody is brilliant and flawless in every way, we are all different from one another; instead of thinking negatively when you feel like you lack information in a particular area, set aside some time to study and acquire the knowledge you need to change your perspective.

Solutions. Remind yourself that you are brilliant in a unique way and that you can learn more about anything you want to instead of thinking you're not smart. You may make lifelong learning one of your ongoing objectives.

9. The fear of not succeeding. It's unfair to have high standards for yourself and to base your sense of value on how well you achieve. If you want diverse outcomes in life, you have to be willing to take risks. Never be afraid to fail; the true failure is never trying.

Solutions. Say to yourself, "I am going to try; I am not scared of failing; that is not what is important," when facing a difficult circumstance or risk. Nothing is truly a failure as long as you learn anything about the world and yourself, even if you "fail."

10. Negative things will occur. Thinking negatively means assuming that the worst-case scenario will occur in any situation. If you visualize the best-

case scenario instead, how would it feel? Our optimistic and negative thoughts have great power, and visualizing the best-case scenario is a typical visualization technique.

You impact your outcomes regardless of whether you envision the worst-case or the best-case situation. Put more emphasis on the things you want to happen and less on what you don't want.

Solutions. Try considering the best-case scenario when you try anything rather than the worst-case scenario. This will help you aim high and go further than you did previously, even if you fall somewhat short.

In brief. Everybody occasionally has unpleasant thoughts. On the other hand, your happiness is compromised when the majority of your thoughts are negative. Our thoughts directly impact our emotions, which in turn influence our actions.

To improve your mental health and put yourself back on the path to positivity if you're depressed and experiencing an overwhelming amount of negative thoughts.

Don't place restrictions on your potential or yourself. Take control of your ideas to alter your outcomes.

Making Our Dream Journal and Vision Board

A vision board is an actual physical manifestation of our goals and dreams. It's a word, image, and symbol collage that helps us visualize the life we wish to lead. Making a vision board is a potent practice that enhances the benefits of creative visualization.

The Craft of Curation

Start by compiling phrases and images expressing your vision board goals. These might be magazine images, quotations, or any other visuals that conjure up the emotions connected to your dreams. Choosing these pictures is a creative visualization process in and of itself.

Organize the pictures on a board in a way that speaks to you and is visually appealing. Your vision board ought to be an artistic creation that embodies your aspirations.

The Ability to Visualise

After creating your vision board, hang it up somewhere you'll see it daily. Every time you view it, pause to fully immerse yourself in the pictures and experience the feelings they arouse. Permit yourself to think that you are already receiving these desires.

Reinforcing the pictures in your head. It improves the effectiveness of manifestation by bringing your subconscious into line with your conscious objectives.

Keeping a Journal on Our Manifestation Path

A dream journal is a hallowed place to document your journey towards manifestation. It serves as a storehouse for your ideas, insights, and experiences as you pursue your goals. Maintaining a dream journal enables you to track your development, obtain understanding, and establish a stronger bond with your dreams.

The Process of Introspection

Write down your goals and objectives to start your dream notebook. Give a thorough description, using words to create a mental picture. Your intentions are strengthened by this reflective act, which is a type of creative visualization.

Continue to regularly add to your dream notebook as you travel through life, recording your experiences, ideas, and revelations. Take note of any coincidences, encouraging signals, or serendipitous events that arise. These posts are a documentation of your journey and an example of the effectiveness of manifestation.

Gratitude and Confirmation

Incorporate thankfulness and affirmations into your dream diary. Affirmations that uphold your goals and beliefs should be written down. For instance, if you want to draw abundance, you could write, "I am open to receiving abundance in all forms."

Gratitude expression is a potent exercise that supports optimistic thinking. Even before your dreams come true, sit down and write down all the things you have to be thankful for. Having gratitude makes you more in tune with the universe's abundance.

We paint the dream tapestries using creative imagination and visualization as the brushes and palettes. By bringing our ambitions to life through vision boards and dream journals, we reaffirm our goals and fortify our faith in the manifestation process. We are the curator and the artist in the gallery of our minds, creating the masterpiece that is our life.

A MindsetOf Abundance And Gratitude

There's an endless dance between abundance and gratitude in the great ballroom of the human heart. It's a waltz of the soul, a tuneful duet that ushers in a world of plenty while transcending the limitations of lack.

The Dancing of Plenty

The Secret to Abundance: Gratitude

Gratitude is the key that unlocks the vault of limitless riches hidden inside the wealth of life. It is a transformational energy, a magical incantation that multiplies blessings and reveals the treasures buried in plain sight rather than merely a courteous "thank you" for life's gifts.

Gratitude is the prism through which we view the beauty of the world. It is the recognition of the little miracles in life, such as the feel of the sun on our skin, the sound of loved ones laughing, or the simple joy of a shared meal. It is the understanding that despite difficulties, there is always something to be grateful for.

The power of thankfulness to change our viewpoint makes it so beautiful. It shifts our attention from what we need to what we already have. We learn from this change that abundance is a mentality rather than a physical state. Realizing that life is about appreciating what we have rather than trying to have it all is what it is all about.

By embracing thankfulness, we establish a magnetic field that draws in additional benefits from life. Our gratitude is met with abundant possibilities, love, and joy from the cosmos. Gratitude is the magic that turns difficulties into opportunities and shortages into plenty.

However, thankfulness is not just found in life's great gestures; it also flourishes in the small, quiet moments that make up each day. The chart that guides us to the gold of contentment is the treasure. The more we find wealth in life's simplicity, the more thankfulness we cultivate.

Gratitude serves as our mooring when things are turbulent and unpredictable. It serves as a reminder that there are moments of brightness even in the middle of the storm. Head-on because we are aware of our many gifts.

Gratitude is an endless source of abundance rather than a limited resource. It is the poetry of our life, the tune that sings in our hearts. The key opens the door to a fulfilling life of meaning and purpose.

The Chemistry of Appreciation

Gratitude is a powerful force that transforms our world, not merely a kind way to say "thank you." We may access the limitless flow of abundance when we dance with gratitude. This is transforming the commonplace into the remarkable—the alchemy of thankfulness.

The link that connects our desires to their realization is gratitude. We may express to the universe our gratitude for what we already have and our openness to receiving more through the language of our hearts. The hint of recognition is what turns fleeting moments into enduring treasures.

Converting Plenty Into Scarcity

Scarcity is the perception that there is not enough and one lives in a constrained world. It is a shadow that many people carry around with them. It's as though you're looking at life's enormous feast through a small window and are certain there won't be enough for everyone. It's the idea that we are nothing more than beggars in the vast marketplace of life.

The startling surprise is that the enchantment starts when we resist scarcity. It seems like the cosmos is working against us, flipping a cosmic switch. Abundance suddenly erupts from the universe, and life's color palette becomes wildly colorful.

Transitioning from scarcity to abundance is enlightening, awakening our senses to the buried riches around us. It's realising that life is a lavish dinner rather than a small snack, a vast carnival of experiences waiting to be enjoyed.

The most unexpected finding is that our resources increase as we give more. We discover that the cosmos continues to fill our cup even more when we reach out to assist others, proving that abundance is not a limited resource. The more we give in this contradictory dance, the wealthier we become.

We find the key to generosity in the shift from scarcity to plenty. This is the golden thread that ties us to the complexities of human nature. It's recognising that kindness, love, and compassion are abundant and multiply when given.

However, the fact that abundance is more than just a reflection of financial prosperity may be the most startling realization of all. It's a mentality, a feeling of satisfaction, an awareness that we already have plenty of relationships, love, and thankfulness.

Be ready for amazement when you decide to take on this alchemical trip. Observe how the surroundings change and the hidden gems of life's plenty become visible. When you change your viewpoint, the concept of scarcity will vanish from your mind, and you will be overcome with wonder at the utter beauty of life.

Sleeplessness and overthinking

Chronic sleeplessness is one of the most debilitating consequences of overthinking. A sleep issue that persists for more than one month is called insomnia. Prolonged sleeplessness is a significant issue. It may result in a higher chance of:

a stroke

Convulsions

weakeneddefenses against diabetes

elevated blood pressure

Heart conditions

Sleep deprivation can cause extreme weariness, which increases your chance of falling or becoming injured in an accident. It can also exacerbate mental health issues, including despair, anxiety, and disorientation. Of course, overthinking is not the only cause of insomnia. Even things like nutrition and stress can impact how well you sleep, but they usually only cause short-lived, acute episodes of insomnia that last one or two nights.

Chronic insomnia, especially onset and maintenance insomnia, is linked to overthinking. When you have insomnia from the beginning, you have trouble falling asleep. While overthinking is the problem, this usually means that your mind races while you try to sleep, regardless of how exhausted you are. You may start dwelling on unfavorable ideas and anxieties regarding the future. When you have maintenance insomnia, you could wake up from sleep abruptly and frequently feel nervous and agitated, even though there might not be a clear reason for your inability to sleep. You have a really hard time falling back asleep once you are awake.

The two forms of sleeplessness are just as dangerous. If overthinking is the root cause of your insomnia, using positive thinking strategies will improve your sleep quality. In Chapter 9, you'll find advice on how to deal with insomnia.

Chapter 3: Mastering Your Critic Within

Everybody has an inner critic—that voice in their heads that constantly critiques their lives. Adopting positive thinking practices and habits can be more challenging if your inner critic is unrelentingly negative. This chapter describes the function of your inner critic, identifies the signals it gives you, and provides strategies for reframing what it says.

Which inner critic are you?

The mental dialogue we all encounter is called your inner critic. It is sometimes called an inner voice communicating with us and is particularly vocal in evaluating our actions. Nothing pleases our inner critic more than to obsess over a mistake or setback. It will never stop telling us that we simply weren't good enough, and that's why everything went wrong. If our inner critic is allowed to run amok, it can cause us to lose confidence in ourselves and our abilities.

In popular psychology, the phrase "inner critic" is frequently employed. It's not an official, scholarly phrase. The inner critic and the Freudian concept of the superego—a mental narrator that mediates and promotes behavior in line with societal norms—are comparable in certain aspects. Generally speaking, the inner critic is far more critical. This annoying inner voice will scrutinize everything we do, focus on mistakes, and downplay our successes. This inner critic can affect even those who appear self-assured and accomplished, causing them to experience guilt and unjustified inadequacy.

Remember the scenario where you took an exam and received a score of 90% from Chapter 1? The part of your brain that obsesses over how you lost that final 10% of your weight rather than applauding your success is known as your inner critic. Fortunately, you can retrain your inner critic to become a more constructive and positive voice.

Inner nurturer versus inner critic

Your inner critic is not the only voice in your head. Additionally, some psychologists refer to you as having an inner nurturer. The internal critic is not this voice. It gives us encouragement and self-compassion and acknowledges our successes. The issue is that the inner critic's voice frequently dominates the inner nurturer's advice and is much louder.

We start to fear making mistakes when the equilibrium between these two inner voices is thrown off, favoring the inner critic. Because we are afraid, we do nothing. However, the only way to succeed and learn is to take action. Our lives are shortened if we allow our inner critic to control us to the point where we are hesitant to attempt anything new or take a chance. Our willingness to work hard and sense of self-worth gradually diminish.

When your inner critic overpowers your inner nurturer, how can you tell? Consider posing the following queries to yourself:

Do you ever lose your temper with yourself? Consider the situation. Was all of this rage justified? Would you have been as upset with someone else if they had done what you did?

Do you ever tell yourself that you're a complete moron or just not good enough, screaming at yourself inside your head? Once more, attempt to step back and consider the circumstances impartially. Did you truly behave foolishly or carelessly?

Have you ever convinced yourself that you are unworthy or a horrible person? These are typical signals coming from a critical inner voice. They're just untrue most of the time.

Your inner critic appears to constantly be prepared to point out how you are falling short of its irrationally high standards. Where is this voice coming from, so negative and insistent?

Managing Disgusting Trauma

An unrelentingly critical inner critic for many people is frequently the result of trauma or other traumatic experiences in the past. Trauma is the emotional reaction to an upsetting circumstance or incident. This can be something you witnessed, something that directly affected you, or even just something you heard or read about (this is known as "vicarious trauma"). Everybody reacts to trauma differently. Some people experience chronic trauma, which can have a long-lasting effect and lead to a variety of issues like overthinking, anxiety, and insomnia. It might also make your inner critic more strong.

The traumatic event or events may have occurred a long time ago, possibly even in your early years, and you might not even be aware that the trauma is still affecting you. Feeling as though you might have avoided the circumstances that led to the trauma is a typical reaction to trauma. Although that perspective is frequently untrue, having such feelings might elicit strong emotions like guilt. We refer to this type of trauma as "shameful trauma."

The duration and intensity of traumatic situations might vary. These can include one-time violent crimes, sexual assault, abuse, and even what appear to be longer-lasting but less severe traumas. An unsupportive and negative parent who doesn't change can be a traumatizing factor. It doesn't matter what causes the embarrassing trauma to begin. How it impacts you is what counts. The first step in lessening the effects of such trauma is to intentionally confront the experience. You might find it helpful to work through the second activity, "Creating a trauma narrative," in Chapter 9.

Trauma might limit your capacity for positive thinking by amplifying the voice of your inner critic. Trauma may be the source of the inner critic's voice for certain individuals.

You might even recognize the voice of your inner critic as one from your past if you pay close attention. For example, it could be the voice of an uncaring father, a competing sibling, or an exacting and critical instructor. Its impact can be mitigated by paying attention to the voice and understanding the trauma it stems from.

Trauma frequently stems from early life experiences. Writing a letter to yourself as a child is a useful strategy for dealing with this. Chapter 9 has instructions on how to accomplish this.

Section Two

Mentality

We should approach our trip in these modern realities with the appropriate perspective. Without the right mindset, reaching your goals in life is impossible because they form the basis for all you do. How can you properly prepare your mentality? This has a lot of significance. Packing wisely is crucial when starting a trip to make sure you have everything you need and don't bring needless items. Since our thoughts create our reality, the first place to start is within your mind. Keeping your thoughts in order will guarantee safe and steady travel. Making a distinction between negative and good factors should be your first step. Imagine it as if you were holding a mental sieve and sorting the important grains from the others. These elements may vary, more or less, depending on the individual. But let's also look for universal components that people experience, considering the mechanics of influence—a topic we shall cover in later chapters.

First and foremost, it is advisable to have emotional equilibrium in the head. I advise deciding for your life. What sort of person would you like to live your life as? Do you want to engage with others positively, or would you rather erect barriers and treat them badly because, for example, you disagree with their appearance, origin, or beliefs? People are trained to have labels, which severely restricts our options for action. Tolerance is taught to kids in schools these days, even at an early age. Young minds are conditioned to accept that treating someone less fortunate than yourself based only on physical characteristics—such as skin color—is unacceptable from the moment they are exposed to this concept. The governing system divides society this way—the word "tolerance" contradicts itself. Recall that nothing is real; everything is just a concept. These ideas shape our reality. Therefore, doors lead to a different, friendlier world where everything is conceivable as long as you let it, and it serves the greater good if you have a clear mind. If both of you allow it, even your biggest foe can become your closest friend. This is but one illustration. We will go into more detail on how to approach people.

People, including myself and you, build our world by causing events. As a result, your attitude to others should be consistent with your initial mindset. Most of us have undoubtedly made quick decisions about someone before. I'll confess that I've frequently had unfavorable thoughts about people before getting to know them, just to find out later that they're good people. When you judge someone before getting to know them, you create an environment in which they are less likely to react positively to you. You can use your ideas to start a sequence of events. Naturally, you can trust your intuition and your "higher self" when you meet someone new, but you should also make it a habit to avoid passing judgment. Due to a pessimistic and misinformed perspective, our lives may appear chaotic when we don't know much. Despite outward appearances, "life" is something we must learn about and comprehend. Avoiding passing judgment on and criticizing other people is a basic habit we should cultivate. You'll be surprised at how much more space your mind has to breathe when you stop judging and criticizing everyone and everything. There are two outcomes when you judge everything. First, you fill your mind with pointless things, which lowers your resonance frequency with the surroundings and, in turn, lessens your ability to be creative and have a nice day, even if just somewhat. Second, you set off a series of circumstances that could result in you receiving criticism or being unfairly assessed if you criticize someone out loud or in your mind. Your own energy is reflected to you in a mirrored form. As a result, it's imperative to break the practice of passing judgment on others, calling attention to their errors, or making fun of their shortcomings.

The person who chastised them could just as easily suffer the same fate as someone else. The process of sending the energy that has been created back to the source, known as the karmic system, is always exact and flawless. I advise you to revise your strategy to create favorable situations in your life. Examine yourself first before scrutinizing others. Consider your personality and the way you would act in various circumstances. Since none of us are flawless, let's begin by noting who we are. Those who are psychologically weaker and who utilize these behaviors to "heal" their fears should be left to receive criticism and judgment.

After realizing this, I tried my best to avoid passing judgment on or criticizing other people or things. Why? Because these life conditions arise more frequently, we participate in these behaviors. And in a circumstance like this, what occurs? You can make fun of someone ten times and laugh heartily, but eventually, you'll find yourself in a different setting and crying—not from laughter. They vanish from your life as soon as you stop transmitting these kinds of vibrations with your mind. Put simply, your life is determined by the thoughts you entertain. Therefore, consider twice before unjustly criticizing someone. Each issue can be approached uniquely. We will talk about the best way to achieve that objective. For the time being, as they say, don't judge a book by its cover. By the way, proverbs are a goldmine of insightful information if you look closely at them. Teaching the origins of words and names and the meanings of proverbs should be a separate subject in elementary schools.

I'm just putting this as a side remark. You can keep saying things like, "Too many cooks spoil the broth," or "He who digs a pit for others falls into it himself" forever. Let go of judgment and evaluation, and your life will become easier. You can watch what's going on but don't label what you see since it will prevent you from coming up with other options.

Figurative language, or how we speak and think, is another part of our worldview that must be reevaluated. Keep in mind that life is life itself. Because of the strength of the Entity's intellect above us, we survive, and our cells haven't broken down. That's how it appears to me, at least. Remember that the Programmer hears what you're thinking and understands how to react to what you're conjuring, even if you don't say anything aloud but think it through in your thoughts. It's a working mechanism that just needs us to be able to tell what's right for us from wrong. It doesn't need any calculations from us. What does it mean to maintain good language use? I mean, I'm talking about swearing, bad attitudes, and body language. The proper frequency of incidents correlates with the resonance of offensive words. Several contexts exist, but the mere existence of certain terms diminishes our worth. I can attest from personal experience that while it's easy to say, it's not always easy to do. I began to observe two ways that people communicate with me throughout my teens. One was the community's common vocabulary, while the other was a respectful way of speaking to one another. I am not referring to discussions with relatives or shop employees but rather with important strangers.

Slang was used frequently in my speech when I was among friends or in a classroom setting. Put differently, you must caw like a crow when you're among them. I also found that I rarely used foul language in our chats with someone I regarded as a valuable outsider, such as an older and well-respected acquaintance or someone with whom I had closer financial ties. I recalled that incident that introduced me to strong language and showed me how to have this kind of conversation. I was born in the 1980s, and the first time I heard the line from the Polish film "Psy" (which is also known as "Dogs" in English), I was about ten years old. At least not to the extent that I had in that movie; I had never heard language like that before. We observe what is going on in the film and television industries nowadays. A TV show or movie may not air because of the low audience if it doesn't contain sexual scenes. Even in this day and age, prime-time television hosts occasionally let themselves use offensive language when they are presenting on public networks. Today's parents are frequently too busy or not much better than the ones in the film "Psy," as a result, kids pick up questionable life skills. Where should they get their role models if not from public personalities or television? The jargon derived from today's "super" works is only made worse by schools.

Before I give two anecdotes, let me add something. I don't pretend to be a saint, but I'm not one either. I admit that I occasionally swear, but there's a reason for it. It's because almost all of us were raised in this manner by commercial means. Everyone has experienced this at some point, whether on TV, in school, on the street, or at home, and it has become deeply embedded in our routines. Depending on your age, we are already relics, as I have said on occasion. Even if those are only numbers, I'm more like forty than twenty. The upbringing of our new generation and our heirs will determine the course of the future. We have the chance to impart elegant communication skills and appropriate language to our kids. We didn't have this chance, some could argue. Now that we are more conscious of the situation, we ought to create a future and a world with completely different values for our kids. I'm not perfect, and I sometimes make mistakes in front of my kids for various reasons. But now that kids are older, I can teach and explain why this behavior is inappropriate.

Moreover, my kids are smart enough to know the difference between right and wrong. They are strictly prohibited from using foul language, and I'm happy with the situation as it stands right now. I would argue that someone is incorrect if they believe they can curse in front of their kids and still appear pious. As was mentioned, this takes us back to a few paragraphs previously. Don't pass judgment or offer criticism. Rather than pretending that such things don't exist and avoiding discussions on this topic, it is far better for youngsters to face such language at home, explain it to them clearly, grasp what depends on it, and understand why it's improper. To a greater or lesser degree, every parent understands that although you can raise your kids at home and read them lovely poems, eventually, they will need to go to school, where they will encounter a variety of parental concerns that will be passed on to their amazing kids. For instance, my child befriended a student at school who subsequently revealed to have a vulgar father. Every scenario included the usage of profanity, including birthday celebrations at home and when driving other kids about. Since we cannot shield our kids from everything, some subjects are best discussed and concluded at home. Of course, it is untrue if someone believes that their home is filled with such language on a daily basis. I'm referring only to circumstances that result from particular partnerships. It seems like my child has made a buddy at school, but I won't let them visit his house because his father is rude.

..Verses

Repetition of positive statements creates an absolute confidence in your mind, which is what affirmations are. We are inundated with messages daily—from TV, newspapers, and magazines, among other media—that we are insufficient. We cannot have it that we will never be as excellent as "them." etc.

Remember that TV ad where a young, attractive man with six-pack abs was surrounded by six girls, or the one where a model walked the red carpet looking flawless, or the one where a celebrity showed up in his Lamborghini to a sexy party?

Even if it seems innocuous, this exposure makes regular men and women wonder who they are. It quietly establishes a "standard" that individuals feel they will never be able to meet.

This diminishes our self-assurance and faith in our talents.

We also need to combat it. We must RECLAIM our self-worth and confidence.

Here's where affirmations come in very handy. Your daily affirmations will serve as a helpful reminder of your worth and ability. It's going to be your confidence "boost" for the day. It will shield your self-assurance from all kinds of bullshit that is directed at you.

Athletes such as Lady Gaga, Will Smith, Jim Carrey, Oprah Winfrey, and Arnold Schwarzenegger attest to the power of affirmations.

Affirmations indeed work, but only when applied appropriately. After four years of practicing affirmations, I can genuinely state that they have greatly influenced my life.

Appropriate Ways To Do Affirmations?

1) Put your fears and uncertainties in writing on paper. Next, list the five biggest fears and concerns preventing you from moving forward.

2) After you've listed the five largest doubts you have, list the exact opposite affirmative assertion. A positive remark that counters a doubtful assertion, such as "I don't deserve to be rich," could be, "I fully deserve to be rich."

Convert each of your five doubts into a positive statement that contradicts it. Put them in writing.

Ensuring that every affirmation you use is positive and in the current tense is important. Avoid making future-focused statements such as "I will succeed in the future" or "I will have a fit body." These statements fall into the "maybe in future" category in your thoughts.

The present tense and positivity are required in your affirmations. Example: I have abundance in my life, I am successful, I deserve wealth, and my body is in good shape. Do you get it? Upbeat and in the present tense.

3) After you have transformed your five negative ideas into five positive ones on paper, list the additional five positive beliefs you feel will be most beneficial to you. This is the kind of thinking you should have—these five

principles. I am an excellent learner, for instance. I can handle any circumstance.

4) As of right now, you have ten affirmations that you wish to live by. Five of your negative beliefs were transformed into positive ones. And five more that you believe are necessary. Now is the time to instill these ten ideas in your thoughts. Position yourself in front of a mirror, ideally one that allows you to see your entire body and fix your gaze directly into the mirror.

5) Aloud, recite your affirmations. Ensure you deliver them with passion and emotion as if you genuinely believe them. You can evoke feelings using gestures and facial expressions when

making assertions. This is a crucial matter.

Say it with genuine sincerity, for instance, if you affirm, "I am going to be a millionaire." Adjust your alignment. Assume a proud stance with your chest out in front of you. Raise both hands and exclaim "YES!" with a victorious tone. Now, say your affirmation aloud twice more.

Make every effort to include feeling in your affirmations. Emotionally charged statements have a profound impact on our thinking.

The significance of incorporating emotion into your affirmations is emphasized by Dr. Joseph Murphy (author of the best-selling book "The

Power of Your Subconscious Mind") and success coach Anthony Robbins (author of "Unlimited Power" and "Awaken The Giant Within"). You wouldn't get any benefit from doing affirmations for years without it.

Practice your affirmations every day. It simply takes five minutes, and you will see a change in your behavior in two to three weeks. Keep repeating these affirmations, and they will become ingrained in your thoughts.

This method has helped me alter my ideas and is quite effective. All you have to do is commit to it. Don't consider if it will succeed or fail. Put aside your doubt and give it a shot for a while. You won't want to stop once you begin to perceive the distinction.

3. Illustration

The term "visualisation" simply means "imagined in great detail" or "vivid imagination."

It's a really powerful method for altering your views. Medical science has demonstrated that the mind cannot distinguish between reality and a vivid imagination.

In one experiment, an athlete was asked to visualize running on a track as precisely as possible while scanners were attached to his body. According to scanner data, his muscles were firing during visualization, similar to when he was jogging on a track.

Numerous research types have since confirmed visualization's beneficial impact on an individual's real performance. This is now a well-established truth in sports psychology, and trainers emphasize the importance of consistent mental practice in addition to physical practice.

This is where it gets interesting: we now understand how beliefs are formed and strengthened by "real-life evidence."

Your subconscious mind cannot distinguish between detailed imagination and real life, so you may use visualization to give it any "evidence" it wants.

Your mind will accept a scenario that you can picture clearly as real. This means you can "manufacture" evidence to support your positive thoughts.

This is an extremely potent idea with practically endless potential. Let's say you suffer from social anxiety. You're anxious about approaching strangers at a party and striking up a conversation. Your mind will soon accept it as reality, and your social anxiety will significantly lessen if you imagine for ten to fifteen minutes that you are at a party full of strangers and are at ease while mingling with them.

I overcame my anxiety about public speaking by using visualization. I've had a lot of unpleasant public speaking situations in the past. On stage, I used to stammer, lose my line of thought, and wonder what other people thought of me. It was very awkward.

However, after learning about visualization and its principles, I decided to try it. Thus, I closed my eyes the night before my major presentation and imagined myself speaking in front of an audience.

I experienced the same nervousness as when I walked on stage. It felt almost the same. However, I made myself give my speech as well as I could. Because I was seeing things in my head, I would pause every time I made a mistake, try to do it again, and hope for perfection.

I had to practice visualization fifteen times before I was able to virtually eliminate my nervousness throughout the speech.

It felt familiar when I finally stepped onto the stage the following day. Like I'd done it previously. While I did experience "some" anxiety, it was easily controlled. After my speech, several approached me to compliment me on how effectively I had communicated my point.

Chapter 4: Step #3: Develop Your Ability to Make Decisions

Developing a positive outlook and problem-solving skills is the first step toward enhancing your decision-making abilities. There are everyday decisions in life that you make without giving them much thought, but there are other decisions that call for greater thought. These choices frequently involve alternatives, complexity, uncertainty, high-risk outcomes, and interpersonal problems.

You must assess the advantages and disadvantages of the various options accessible to you, comprehend them closely, and consider various decision-related factors. Additionally, you must ascertain the nature of the event, uncover any undiscovered information about the decision, and forecast the responses and reactions of various parties involved.

You need to put your problem-solving and decision-making hat on when dealing with such complicated challenges to make sure you choose the optimal course of action given the circumstances and the options at your disposal.

Now, let's talk about the methodical technique you may use to make wise choices to improve your situation and solve your problems.

Create A Structural Area Around You

As of February 2018, Kenneth Langone, one of the Home Depot founders, stated, "You need to surround yourself in an environment where the best minds are found." He uses Home Depot, his company, as an example. Home Depot is one of the biggest retailers of home improvement products, employing 400,000 people and operating over 2200 sites across North America. He once claimed that the culture they fostered is what makes them successful. He used a triangle to illustrate this future, with the newly hired employee at the base and the company's CEO typically at the top. Unfortunately, businesses rarely pay attention to the person at the bottom. However, Home Depot decided to flip the triangle, calling on recently hired employees to inquire about any ideas they may have on improving the store.

Everyone feels like they are a team member in the atmosphere that Home Depot has created. This setting makes it simple for them to make decisions that will help the business expand.

Having a supportive environment that facilitates effective choice-making makes decision-making easier. The individuals involved in the process and the locations you choose to make decisions make up your environment. Here are some other tips to enhance your surroundings so you can make wise decisions:

To help you focus on the issue and think clearly, make sure your workspace is calm, quiet, and distraction-free. Choose a quiet place to make a personal decision if you must. If at all feasible, choose a calm, cozy space in your home for yourself to reflect.

Make sure you gather all the data and supporting documentation for the choice you must make, and keep the pertinent documents in that room so you can review them thoroughly and quickly while evaluating the choice. You'll benefit from this in two ways: first, you'll be able to respond swiftly, and second, you'll feel much more confident as you proceed.

As indicated in the Home Depot example, consider the individuals engaged in the process and, if necessary, make a list of them. Whether it's for professional or personal reasons, ask everyone who matters to join you on the journey. Ask your partner to come along if it's a family choice that needs their approval and input. When tackling a business-related issue, conduct a thorough stakeholder analysis to identify the stakeholders who need to be included and ask for their assistance. Time is frequently wasted during decision-making processes involving an excessive number of participants. To prevent it, give everyone the pertinent and crucial information about the circumstance and request that each person analyze it in-depth. After that, they can come to you with recommendations and choices, which you can compare to other viewpoints.

Gather All Necessary Data

Never base a judgment on incomplete knowledge. Do as much research as possible on the issue and gather all relevant data, no matter how little. Start by doing extensive web research on the issue, and if necessary, move on to a market study. Consider the opinions of specialists and others connected to the issue as well. For example, if you are concerned about how to fund your firm, ask a buddy who works in finance for suggestions on how to attract investors to your initiative.

If you are making a personal choice, you should still do your homework, read books, and seek advice from experts in the field or from people who have accomplished comparable or related goals. For instance, if you are considering relocating to a different city to pursue your ideal career, speak with your highly ambitious aunt and get her advice. Though you don't have to follow her advice, you should at least consider her advice to make an informed choice.

Apply the CATWOE Technique

A useful analytical method for thoroughly evaluating a situation and selecting the optimal course of action is CATWOE Analysis. Customer, Actor, Transformation, Weltanschauung, Owner, and Environment are the acronyms for these words. Let's take a closer look at these variables:

Customer: The people who receive the results are referred to here. Determine who will be most impacted by the choice, whether business-related or personal. If it's your clients, consider things from their perspective and perhaps survey your intended audience. When making decisions that affect your staff, get their input and imagine yourself in their position. Consider what the other person might want out of the circumstance while making decisions about your family or relationship.

Actor: This describes the roles involved in carrying out the decision-related procedures. When making a business-based decision, consider how the employees will behave. Everyone who will be a part of the decision-making process must be considered. Ask your family for advice if you're considering relocating to a different nation. They will be involved in the process, and it won't be easy to adjust if they don't work with you.

Transformation: The fundamental procedure yields the desired result. When deciding whether or not to pursue an MBA, consider the time commitment, the courses you will need to take, and the effort that will be required. You'll be able to determine whether or not it is worth your time and effort after you better understand the time, effort, money, and other resources you will need to devote to achieve the desired results.

Global Perspective: It alludes to the fundamental values and beliefs influencing the choice. It is important to analyze the greater picture, the rationale behind your consideration of a particular course of action, the issue you are attempting to solve, and the wider implications and influence surrounding the problem and likely resolution. If you're considering switching from a legal career to a fashion design one, think about why you feel driven to do so, the goal you want to achieve, and why you can't give up on it.

Owner: This is the interested party or stakeholder most impacted by the decision and has the most influence. You will be the direct owner of any decision, whether it is personal or professional and relates to you. Examine your requirements, desires, goals, interests, abilities, and emotions about the choice when examining this component. To make sure you move forward appropriately, ask yourself questions like "What is it that I want?" "What brings me true meaning and value?" "What am I trying to achieve?" "What is in it for me?" "How does that affect me?" "What is my purpose?" and other questions along these lines.

Environment: The limitations, considerations, and guidelines that surround the choice. Examine the regulations about the product and the setting of your enterprise when deciding on its launch. When making a personal choice, consider the impact of your present surroundings.

This method assists you in determining and evaluating each individual and element associated with the choice to make the least risky choice possible.

Step 2: Select the Time and Location

The next thing you should do is establish a morning, lunch break, or even evening routine that you can stick to.

Pick a peaceful, comfortable location where you can concentrate on journaling without interruptions. Some ideas include your bedroom, a coffee shop, or a quaint area of your house.

Step 3: Decide What You Want

You should take some time to establish your intentions for the journaling session before you even begin. Consider the objectives you have for your journaling. Here are a few instances:

Thinking back on recent experiences or occurrences

Managing challenging feelings

generating concepts for specific tasks or objectives

expressing appreciation or happiness

You may maintain your motivation and focus during your journaling exercise by setting an intention.

Step 4: Get Writing

It's time to get writing now. You can use the following strategies and pointers to make the most of your journaling:

Grammar, spelling, and punctuation are not important. Simply allow your ideas to come to you without editing or judgment.

Don't hide or minimize your emotions. Permit yourself to be open and, above all, genuine.

Write down the current topics on your mind and your current ideas. Avoid worrying about the past or the future.

Try journaling in various ways, such as using art, bullet, or reflective journals.

Step 5: Consider and Evaluate

After finishing, set aside some time to consider all you have written down. What fresh insight did you gain about who you are? What realizations or understandings did you gain? By thinking back on your writing, you can get ideas.

Think about going back and reading what you wrote from time to time. In this manner, you can monitor your development, spot reoccurring problems or tendencies, and acknowledge your successes and personal improvement.

Thank You

Having gratitude is appreciating all of life's blessings, no matter how minor.

Combining mindfulness with thankfulness gives you a strong tool for building relationships, reducing stress, and cultivating happiness.

In 2016, Y. Joel Wong and other scientists from Indiana University Bloomington's Department of Counseling and Educational Psychology published a paper in Psychotherapy Research.

Two hundred ninety-three persons undergoing therapy participated in an experiment by the researchers. Three groups of participants were formed. First, there was the control group, which got nothing except treatment. In addition to receiving treatment, the second group journaled about their inner feelings and ideas on the traumatic events they went through. The third group wrote letters to people expressing their gratitude and got therapy.

The researchers discovered that after the 12-week intervention, the participants who wrote letters of thanks said they felt better than the other two groups. This demonstrates how writing down your gratitude can improve your mental health and be a helpful component of therapy.

But there was a fascinating turn of events. The researchers discovered that their feelings worsened when participants wrote with unpleasant, emotive language. The improvement was not as great for those who focused on writing down negative emotional terms as it was for the ones who wrote down gratitude.

According to this study, adding letter writing or thankfulness exercises to treatment may improve mental health.

The following are some advantages of practicing mindfulness and gratitude:

Focusing on and mindfully relishing the positive aspects of your life might help you feel happier and more content with yourself.

Things other than negative thoughts and worries when you practice mindfulness and gratitude.

Relationships can be strengthened and improved by practicing mindfulness in your interactions with people and expressing gratitude.

Gratitude has been connected to reduced blood pressure, a stronger immune system, improved physical health, and improved sleep.

How to Express Gratitude in a Mindful Way

Now that you know its advantages, let's show you how to practice mindful thankfulness. The following actions can help you begin incorporating it into your everyday routine:

Commence with consciousness

Recognizing the blessings in your life is the first step towards cultivating mindful gratitude. Take a moment to consider your blessings, such as a wonderful dinner, a stunning sunset, or a helpful friend.

● Train Your Mind to Appreciate the Present

Once you've found one thing for which you are thankful, use mindfulness to relish it. Take every feeling and detail, and permit yourself to enjoy the whole experience.

● Show Your Appreciation

Don't hold back when speaking. Tell others how much you appreciate them and express your thanks. You might send a short letter or a smile. By expressing your thankfulness, you'll improve your relationship and encourage others.

Iterate Frequently

Like any habit, cultivating mindful thankfulness involves time and repetition. Include it in your everyday schedule. Every day, set aside a little period to think about your blessings and practice mindfulness in the present.

You can utilize mindfulness as a potent tool to enhance your pleasure and well-being while lowering worry and anxiety. By practicing breathing, bodily awareness, mindful communication and activities, self-compassion, acceptance, and letting go of control and perfectionism, you can develop a stronger feeling of being in the present.

Successful Visualization Techniques

One effective technique for bringing the Law of Attraction and the power of positive thinking to life is visualization. You can access your subconscious mind, which houses your emotions and beliefs, and develop a more convincing image of what you want by envisioning achievement. By adopting visualization, you may increase your self-assurance, drive, and concentration, which will help you reach your objectives more quickly.

Imagining yourself accomplishing your goals while closing your eyes is a mental rehearsal known as visualization. It is visualizing your goals in clear, precise detail and going through the associated feelings and emotions as though you've already accomplished them. By using visualization, you may rewire your limiting beliefs and replace them with empowering ones, unlocking the potential of your subconscious mind.

Here are some pointers for successfully utilizing visualization:

1. Schedule time each day.

You must develop the practice of visualizing for it to be a useful tool. Every day, set aside a short period to imagine your goals. It can happen in the morning, before bed, or during your midday meal. Prioritize it and follow through on it.

2. Draw a crisp image

When you visualize your objectives, make a vivid, detailed, and understandable picture. To create a multisensory experience, use your senses. Envision the sights, sounds, tastes, scents, and sensations that come with accomplishing your objectives. Try to make the image as realistic as you can.

3. Pay attention to the good

When you visualize, concentrate on your desires rather than your distastes. Concentrate on the joy and satisfaction that come from accomplishing your objectives. Avert self-doubt and negative self-talk. Have faith that your goals have already been attained.

4. Make use of affirmations

Strong declarations called affirmations might support you in reaffirming your good thoughts. Affirmations such as "I am confident and successful," "I am worthy of success," or

"I am focused and driven" can be used to reinforce your visualization. While you're visualizing, repeat these.

5. Frequently visualize

Although visualization is a potent tool, its effectiveness depends on its regular application. Make sure you are consistent and include it in your everyday routine. It will become more automatic the more you practice.

6. Make use of meditation guides

Visualizing your goals might be aided by guided meditations. Many of them are free and may be found online. These meditations lead you on a trip that facilitates the development of a clear picture of your objectives and the experiences that lead up to them.

7. Use the present tense when visualizing

In your goal visualization, utilize the present tense. Rather than visualizing the journey to your goals, picture yourself there already. This strengthens your image and makes it seem more likely that you have already accomplished your objectives.

8. Show adaptability

When imagining, be adaptable and receptive to several options. Our objectives may occasionally change, or we may discover that a new course is required. While remaining receptive to possibilities, consider the desired outcome.

You can alter your thoughts and beliefs to assist you in reaching your objectives by employing visualization. You'll be astounded at the outcomes if you make it a daily habit, but it does require practice. Gaining more self-assurance, drive, and focus through visualization can help you access the power of your subconscious mind and pave the way for a prosperous and fulfilling life. So, see your desires come true while you picture yourself succeeding.

Why?

He thought back to the lead story he had read. He put the regulation into practice. Before he left the local office the next day, he shared with his fellow sales representatives his disappointments from the previous day. He advised, "Just be on the lookout. I'm going back to the same opportunities today, and I'll sell more insurance than all of you combined!"

The astounding thing is that Al was the one who made it happen. He returned to the same square and called all the people he had spoken to the previous day. He closed 66 new contracts for mishaps!

This was an odd feat of achievement. Moreover, it occurred due to the "awful breaks" when Al walked through wind and storm for eight hours without making a single approach. Al Allen may have changed where he stood. He had the power to transform the negative discontent that most of us would have on a day of relative disappointment into a motivating discontent that led to advancement the next. Al became the company's top sales representative and was promoted to project lead.

For many of our truly fruitful people, this ability to reverse the subtle charm and use the side with the force of PMA instead of the side with the force of NMA is typical. Due to the advantages we lack, most of us will often view Accomplishments perplexingly, maybe because we don't see them, even though we have them. The obvious is frequently hidden. A man's PMA is his advantage; nothing about it is confusing.

After Henry Ford made progress, he became the target of jealousy. People thought Ford's Success was due to karma, strong friends, virtuosity, or whatever "secret" they thought Ford had. Moreover, some of these elements likely adopted a role. But there was more to it than that. Just a handful of people, perhaps one in a thousand, were aware of the true reason for Ford's Success, and those few were usually too shy to talk about it because of how simple it was. One glance at Ford in person will clearly define the "secret."

Many years ago, Henry Ford decided to develop the now-famous V-8 engine. He had to build a motor where each of the eight chambers was cast into a single square. He sent his architects to design just that kind of motor. The architects agreed it was challenging to project an eight-chamber petroleum motor from one piece for one individual.

"Produce it in any case," Portage replied. They replied, "Yet, it is unthinkable."

"Go to work," Ford asked, "and continue to work until you succeed, but long it takes."

The architects got to work. They would have run out of options if they stuck with the Ford employees. After six months, they were still unsuccessful. An extra six months went by with no success. The more the architects tried, the more "incomprehensible" the result looked.

Ford conferred with its architects towards the close of the year. Once more, they informed him they couldn't find a practical way to fulfill his offer. "Just keep working," Ford advised. "I need it, and I will have it."

What was the deal, furthermore?

Considering everything, it was evident that the motor was absolutely practical. The Ford V-8 became the most amazingly productive car on the road, propelling Henry Ford and the company so far ahead of their closest competitor that it took them a long time to make up lost ground. He made use of PMA. Furthermore, you have access to a comparable power. If you apply it and assume that Henry Ford did as well, you too may advance society by bringing the possibility of the impossibly difficult into reality. You can find out how to get what you need, assuming you know what you need.

When a 25-year-old retires at 65, he still has about 100,000 working hours ahead of him. How many hours of labor will you put in under the powerful influence of PMA? More importantly, how many of them will be eliminated by the blinding strokes of NMA?

That being said, how would you allocate more of your life to PMA than to NMA? Some people seem to use this ability without thinking. Henry Ford was always one of them when it came to improving the Ford automobile. Others must learn it. Al Allen progressed by applying and analyzing the information he discovered in books and movement publications. One such book is Accomplishment via a Positive Mental Attitude.

You can also learn how to encourage PMA.

Some people utilize PMA for a while, but after a setback, they stop believing in it. They have a wonderful start, but some "terrible breaks" cause them to reverse the charm. They fail to realize that those who persist in attempting PMA maintain a level of achievement. Their likeness is to the well-known retired racehorse "John P. Grier." John P. Grier was a purebred with exceptional assurance, so much so that he was ready, poised, and charged as the lead pony, capable of defeating the greatest racehorse in history: Man o' Meet the sole surviving person. The day you meet the most important person alive is when you realize PMA for yourself! Who is this guy? Yes, you are the principal living person in the grand scheme of things. Examine yourself. With the initials PMA on one side and NMA on the other, don't you exude an unnoticeable charm? What is this power, this charm exactly? Your soul is the charm. PMA is an optimistic state of mind.

The perfect mental attitude is one of positivity. What kind of mental attitude is ideal? It typically consists of the "in addition to" attributes denoted by terms such as assurance, dependability, faith, good faith, audacity, zeal, open-mindedness, resistance, discernment, generosity, and mental clarity.

NMA is an unfavorable mental attitude. It differs from PMA in several ways.

After focusing on successful men for some time, Positive Mental Attitude led the authors of Success to conclude that having a positive mental attitude is the fundamental mystery they all have in common.

PMA was the key to S. B. Fuller overcoming the negative aspects of being needy. Despite having an injured leg, Tom Dempsey kicked the farthest field goal in a professional football game, thanks to PMA. Furthermore, Henry J. Kaiser's ability to assemble a Liberty Ship like clockwork was undoubtedly fueled by a good mental attitude. Al Allen's ability to upstage his charm convinced him to return to the prospects who had turned him down the day before and break another business record.

Can you figure out how to make your invisible charm work for you? Maybe, maybe not. Perhaps you have developed and reaffirmed your PMA until life grants you all your worthwhile desires. However, if you haven't already, reading this book will help you become proficient with the steps to harness the power of PMA's magic to release the force of PMA in your life.

This book presents a positive mental attitude, explains what it is, and shows how it can be developed and used. It is the one essential principle among the Seventeen Principles in this book that is necessary to achieve significant advancements. A combination of PMA plus at least one of the remaining sixteen levels of achievement is required for Accomplishment. Ace them. As soon as you recall them, start putting them into practice and read Success with an optimistic outlook. If you incorporate all of the guidelines into your life, you will have a positive outlook on life in the most striking way possible.

Additionally, the outcome will be Success, happiness, prosperity, abundance, or any significant goals in daily life. If you possess both the privileges of your colleagues and the laws of infinite knowledge, they will be yours. These kinds of infringement are the most disgusting kinds of NMA.

The formula for maintaining a good outlook in your brain can be found in part two. Master that formula; incorporate it into all you do, and you'll be well to fulfilling your desires.

Establishing A Creative Settlement

It is essential to surround ourselves with an inspiring environment that keeps us motivated and encourages us to keep going when faced with hardship and difficult circumstances. It is impossible to overstate the influence that our environment has on our thoughts, feelings, and general well-being. In this section, we'll look at ways to foster an environment that inspires us, helps us succeed, and helps us overcome whatever challenges we face.

First, we must clear out our mental and physical spaces. Being in a messy space can be exhausting and daunting, making it hard to stay motivated. First, arrange your physical environment, eliminate anything extraneous, and make it tidy and peaceful. This will bring you a clear, concentrated mind and a sense of tranquility.

Additionally, surround oneself with uplifting people. Look for people who are driven, motivated, and have a never-give-up mentality. Talk deeply with people who motivate you, exchange success stories, and give guidance on overcoming obstacles. If you surround yourself with like-minded people, you will be inspired to move forward and continuously reminded of the opportunities ahead.

Apart from individuals, engross oneself in motivational material. Peruse literary works, view films, or tune in to podcasts that explore the experiences of accomplished people who have overcome hardships. Their experiences will serve as a reminder that despite the difficulties, it is always possible to overcome them. Note their approaches, outlook, and fortitude, then incorporate these into your life.

Setting objectives and picturing your accomplishments are additional steps in creating an inspirational atmosphere. Put your objectives in plain sight by hanging vision boards or writing sticky notes on your mirror. Keep yourself inspired by pictures and sayings that speak to your goals and inspire you. You can maintain your resolve and focus in the face of challenges if you remind yourself frequently of your goals.

Finally, develop an optimistic and upbeat internal conversation. Affirmations and constructive self-talk can take the place of negative ideas and self-doubt. Remind yourself of your accomplishments in the past, your strengths, and the difficulties you have already overcome. Maintaining an optimistic outlook can make you more resilient and better able to overcome any challenges that may arise.

In summary, sustaining motivation during difficult times requires the creation of an inspiring atmosphere. We may fuel the fire within and never give up by clearing out our physical and mental space, surrounding ourselves with positive influences, immersing ourselves in inspirational content, picturing success, and developing a positive inner dialogue. Recall that overcoming difficulties determines success, not the lack of them.

Chapter 5: Creating an Inspiring Mentality

Clearly define your objectives and goals.

Having the inner drive to persevere through hardship and difficulties is essential. Establishing specific goals and objectives is the first step in releasing this motivation. You may ignite the fire within and find the drive to conquer any hurdle by identifying your goals and creating a plan.

Clearly defining goals and objectives gives a feeling of purpose and direction. Even in the face of failures, it gives you something to aim for and helps you maintain perspective on the wider picture. Without specific objectives, it's simple to get disoriented, lose motivation, and not know what to do next. By outlining your objectives precisely, you make a successful road plan.

SMART is specified, measurable, achievable, relevant, and time-bound, and this is a crucial consideration while making goals. Having clear objectives can assist you in knowing exactly what you want to accomplish. With measurable objectives, you can monitor your development and recognize your accomplishments. Realistic and attainable objectives ensure you don't put yourself in a position where you will fail. You have a sense of purpose when your goals are relevant and in line with your values and desires. Time-bound objectives have a due date, which makes them feel more urgent and discourages procrastination.

Dividing your goals into more manageable, achievable targets after you have established them is crucial. By acting as stepping stones, these goals help you get closer to your final goal and make it more doable. as you complete each goal by breaking your goals down into smaller activities.

Furthermore, having well-defined goals and objectives helps you maintain accountability. By telling people about your objectives, you stay motivated and hold yourself responsible along the road. These people could be mentors, friends, or relatives. This external accountability might support your motivation through difficult periods.

In conclusion, establishing specific goals and objectives is one of the most important steps in identifying motivation for success. You may feed the fire within and conquer any hardship that comes your way by clearly stating your goals, breaking them down into smaller targets, and communicating your intentions to others. Never forget that it is crucial to maintain focus and determination and never give up throughout difficult circumstances.

Envisioning Achievement and Realizing Your Goals

Finding the drive to never give up is essential throughout tough times. Unexpected obstacles in life can put our resiliency and resolve to the test. All of us, nevertheless, can go past these challenges and succeed. "Visualizing Success and Manifesting Your Dreams," the title of this subchapter, explores the significance of using visualization and manifestation to ignite your inner fire and find success inspiration.

Visualization is an effective technique that lets us picture our desired result in our minds. By visualizing success, we can access the subconscious mind's power and synchronize our beliefs, thoughts, and behaviors with our objectives. We begin to believe in the potential of our dreams coming true when we can picture ourselves accomplishing them. Faced with challenges, visualization keeps us motivated, dedicated and focused on our goals.

Setting clear goals is a necessary first step in the visualizing process. What is it that we want? How does success appear to us? We can visualize our dreams clearly in our minds by providing clear answers to these questions. Seeing, hearing, touching, smelling, and tasting are just a few of the senses we must use to visualize achievement to create a realistic and tangible image. We become fully submerged in this visualization, giving it a rich, emotional quality.

But visualization on its own is insufficient. It needs to be combined with methods for action and manifestation. We begin to draw the possibilities and resources necessary to make our dreams come true when we picture them. This is the point at which manifestation power becomes relevant.

Affirmations, constructive self-talk, and the law of attraction can help us harness the universe's energy to manifest our desires.

It's simple to become discouraged and lose sight of our goals during trying circumstances. But we may feed the fire inside and find inspiration to never give up by implementing manifestation and visualization techniques into our daily lives. By visualizing achievement and making our aspirations come true, we can realize our full potential, triumph over hardship, and lead extraordinary lives.

This section offers direction for anyone looking for inspiration to succeed in life and overcome obstacles.

It provides exercises, doable solutions, and motivational accounts of people who have used manifestation and vision to realize their dreams. After reading this section, readers will acquire the skills and mindset required to rekindle their motivation and overcome any challenge.

Chapter 4: Basic Behavior Modification

Behavioral therapy is a quick and easy approach to start thinking positively and finding happiness.

The basis of behavioral therapy is that unfavorable associations can be changed to positive ones by repeating behavior. The brain learns by creating associations, which our brains do constantly.

With some practice, one can use cognitive behavioral therapy to reinforce positive thinking and attain happiness.

Cognitive behavioral therapy, or CBT, is a useful tool psychologists and therapists use to assist clients in resolving psychological issues. It's also a terrific approach to get rid of negativity.

Using CBT in your positive thinking journey is simple and effective. It is easier to recognize and let go of negativity when you understand why you think and act the way you do.

These methods are streamlined to encourage positive thinking and promote good ones without addressing any underlying psychological problems.

Easy CBT to Promote Positive Thoughts

Refocusing Intentionality

Fundamental Principles

CBT Worksheet

Refocusing

One easy way to practice positive thinking is to refocus. Refocusing helps because, in most cases, negative thoughts require more attention than positive ones.

You have to deliberately try to refocus your mind whenever it starts associating negativity with something by halting the thought and focusing on a positive association instead.

Here's an illustration of refocusing:

You and your closest friend are at odds.

"She always gets angry over such stupid things," is a negative thought.

Feelings: rage and guilt

As a result, you lose a close buddy and don't try to patch things up.

Refocus: "I should apologize; we're both stubborn; I didn't have to get so angry."

Feelings: repentant and tolerant

As a result, you two communicate again and work out your disagreements after your apology.

Refocusing forces you to honestly try to comprehend all sides of a problem.

By conceptualizing both scenarios, you can see the effects of negativity and how a positive shift in emphasis might improve the situation.

Although seeing things from all angles isn't always simple, practicing this skill will help sharpen your attention.

Whatever problem you face, weigh each side's advantages and disadvantages before shifting your attention.

Before you automatically justify both sides, you will need to repeat this process a few times.

The idea is to present both sides with a possible outcome scenario and frame your understanding to assist you in shifting your perspective.

Being mindful

Being aware of your surroundings and in the present moment is the hallmark of mindfulness. Because mindfulness encourages you to pay attention to the people and surroundings, it helps you feel less negative.

Recognize how others respond to you and your actions; remember that not everyone is mindful.

Create a place you enjoy being in by practicing observing your surroundings. Consider your workspace if you work in an office; place a plant on your desk if you enjoy gardening. Try correcting your posture if you find that your chair is unpleasant. Take little breaks from your job to stretch and observe how your body and mind feel.

It is simpler to stop negative ideas when they appear when you engage in mindful practice.

When you act purposefully, it is simpler to notice the little things in life and think positively.

Give your thoughts purpose and practice being aware of everything, including your mood, to avoid letting your mind wander.

A Mindfulness Exercise

Put these three questions in writing, then respond to them each day for a week. This will assist you in realizing how your thoughts and actions are influenced by awareness.

At what number of persons today have you smiled?

Did you laugh how many times today?

Could you describe a nice chat you had today?

Fundamental Principles

Experiences shape your core beliefs, which act as a lens through which you see the world.

There are fundamental ideas in religions, cultures, and people themselves. Your basic beliefs influence how you interpret events. It is challenging to overcome negative core beliefs that underlie negative thoughts and feelings.

It could be challenging at first to identify your personal essential beliefs. Once you've recognized them, you may change them to promote optimistic thinking and assist you in achieving happiness for the rest of your life.

A basic underlying assumption can occasionally distort your entire outlook, making daily life frustrating and, in the end, unbearable. The good news is that those ideas are malleable and can be altered.

The following are some instances of fundamental beliefs and how they can prevent optimistic thinking:

1. Fundamental principle: The strong shall succeed

Negative block: Failure implies weakness. Every time you fall short of your objective, you are more than just a failure; those who fail are also weak.

2. Fundamental conviction: The earth is a heartless place

Untrustworthy people who just think about themselves and assume that others who are compassionate have hidden agendas

3. Central idea: Optimism is naive

Negative block: If someone is hopeful, they will be taken advantage of since hope is foolish and reality is cruel.

You can handle information more positively if you recognize and change your basic negative beliefs. Consider your guiding principles, jot them down, and consider how they have shaped your worldview.

Knowing your fundamental ideas will help you start the process of changing them. You can't just make a positive change; you need to reflect on your views and make meaningful, deliberate, and reasonable changes.

www.ingramcontent.com/pod-product-compliance
Lightning Source LLC
Chambersburg PA
CBHW052133110526
44591CB00012B/1701